HI GOD
I'm Home.
WOW!

BEVERLY WILKINS R.N.

Copyright © 2021 Beverly Wilkins R.N.

All rights reserved. No part of this book may be reproduced, stored, or transmitted by any means—whether auditory, graphic, mechanical, or electronic—without written permission of both publisher and author, except in the case of brief excerpts used in critical articles and reviews. Unauthorized reproduction of any part of this work is illegal and is punishable by law.

This book is a work of non-fiction. Unless otherwise noted, the author and the publisher make no explicit guarantees as to the accuracy of the information contained in this book and in some cases, names of people and places have been altered to protect their privacy.

Scripture taken from the New King James Version®.
Copyright © 1982 by Thomas Nelson. Used by permission.
All rights reserved.

ISBN: 978-1-956373-17-2 (sc)
ISBN: 978-1-956373-18-9 (hc)
ISBN: 978-1-956373-19-6 (e)

Because of the dynamic nature of the Internet, any web addresses or links contained in this book may have changed since publication and may no longer be valid. The views expressed in this work are solely those of the author and do not necessarily reflect the views of the publisher, and the publisher hereby disclaims any responsibility for them.

"HI, GOD. I'M HOME. WOW!"

What if it really *is* birth to birth?

Can you recall that amazing feeling you get when you arrive home after a long trip? You are tired and filled with great memories, but you can hardly wait to walk in your front door, flip off your shoes, and twirl around in your own kitchen, right?

Well, embrace that sensation and hear the dialogue of those who have felt that joy.

I can only imagine that it will be a thousand times greater than even that sensation when we are reborn into the next reality.

Wow. Wow. Thank you, God, for your promise.

> Most assuredly, I say to you, if anyone keeps My Word,
> He shall never taste death. (John 8:51 NKJV)

CONTENTS

Acknowledgments vii
Your Navigation Guide to the End of Your Life ix

Chapter 1   The Invitation 1

Chapter 2   The Grand Plan 4

Chapter 3   The Gift of Death: You Are Still Here, Babby 6
                   The Vision of Spirit 6

Chapter 4   The Wisdom of the Farm 9

Chapter 5   Wisdom of the Children 13

Chapter 6   When is Someone Dead? 15
                   Precious ZarA 16
                   Penelope: Catalyst of Change 17
                   Angela's Gift 18

Chapter 7   The Sound of Death: Whoosh 20

Chapter 8   Visions of Death 23
                   "No. I Don't Want to be Here!" 23
                   The Professor's Revelation 26

Chapter 9   The Nationwide Prayer 29
                   The Catalyst of Story 30

Chapter 10 The Final Goodbye Bell 32
                   Rosie: For Whom the Bell Rings 32

Chapter 11 The Smell of Death 38

Chapter 12 The Spirit Goes On; We Are Light Bodies 43

Chapter 13 Share Your Story 51

Chapter 14 The Final Gift of Choices 52

About the Author 59

ACKNOWLEDGMENTS

I would like to thank all the precious patients throughout my professional career. You have taught me much.

To my dear sister Brenda, who has long listened to many revisions of my thoughts on death and being reborn. She has endured my discussions with many acronyms and sayings like, "Love is not possible without mutual respect," or when evaluating a potential new partner, just ask, "What would Jesus say?" And the real zinger: "The cure for most personal dramas: 'get over yourself.' And the kinder translation: 'Get humble.'"

Thank you to Dr. Alan Wolfelt and his Centre for Loss in Denver, Colorado, for his amazing lifelong wisdom on grief and bereavement.

To my five hundred books and the amazing way they challenged my thinking. From Louise Hay, Deepak Chopra, and Dr. Wayne Dyer to *Out on a Limb* by Shirley McLean, *The Celestine Prophecy*, and *The Four Agreements* to *Conversations with God*. They all authenticate the vision I had on the Pyramid of the Sun in Mexico City in 1969.

To all others, who are trying to elevate the world's thought to another level of consciousness of goodness and kindness to fellow humans.

To my dear parents, Byron and Blanche Bruce, for instilling empathy, independence and resilience with a faith-filled home of two brothers and a sister. I love you all.

To my handsome son, Greg, who now exemplifies a primary family value system with his beautiful wife, Adena, and their three precious children. Thank you for your pragmatic and tender care of me, now that I'm alone. Your love is immeasurable.

Finally, to my late husband and a dear gentleman farmer, Jim, who kept me grounded in love and rural values. Throughout our forty-three years of marriage, we shared adventures and grew in human love. I write about his final gift of farewell, his globe of love, to give others hope in their final goodbye to their spouse or partner. I see him in dancing fireflies and calm moonlit nights and my visiting Jiminy Chipmunk companion.

Finally, to my overall compass, my tattered Holy Bible. These verses ring in my ears when I am confronted with any life dilemma. The answer is always there in the many verses that were imprinted in Sunday school in Ospringe Knox Presbyterian: Psalm 23, Psalm 119, John 3:16, Isaiah, and Revelation. I could have saved a lot of money because many best-selling books retold those many lessons. You permitted me to be an at home missionary through the guise of being a nurse. Thank you, God, for being the Master of my life's ship. I pray to continue to hear your answer when I pray, "Show me the path that Thou wouldst have me take."

This therefore led me to WestBow Press, affiliated with publishing many books sharing the wisdom of Billy Graham. I know that this book is now in God's hands, and I pray it has wings to bring much comfort whenever someone is reborn.

Thanks for all the people I have met.

So glad I invited you into my consciousness.

Keep your wings on.

YOUR NAVIGATION GUIDE TO THE END OF YOUR LIFE

"Hi, God. I'm Home. Wow" is a multisensory guide to the final seconds of your life.

Let's start with some important facts: Death takes one second.

Conversely, the process of getting there is referred to as dying. It starts when you are born, as cells die to be replaced with brand-new ones from that moment forward.

Liver cells are renewed every three hundred days.

Red blood cells degenerate and are replaced every one hundred and twenty days.

Your complete skeleton is replaced every ten years. Skin cells are replaced every thirty-nine days.

Your whole life, you are constantly in a state of replacement.

With each successive birthday, this regeneration starts to slow down, and we age (or erode, as I now call it).

The journey of this book outlines the physical body's pathway to death. It outlines the awareness that I have witnessed through each individual's specific exit; the gift of their final heartbeat and breath.

Chapter 1 welcomes you to the journey. You are invited to determine why you are here to go on this physical lesson at Earth School (thank you, Eckhart Tolle).

Chapter 2 invites you to consider the grand plan that you wished to travel and learn from.

Chapter 3 asks you to understand that death is the final gift you receive. You attempt to learn why you came here to elevate your enlightenment level. Is the gift then to be done with your task and therefore no more pain or consequence of poor choices? Death is the gift; a juxtaposition of words. You can graduate.

Chapters 4 and 5 outline some of the background that I built the foundation of my belief system on, from fundamental truths and realities of the balanced cycle of life on a farm to the innocence and wisdom of the world seen through the eyes of a child.

Chapter 6 examines when death occurs and shows the vision of some of my messengers, from an infant victim of physical and emotional abuse to the reassurance of a six-year-old rejoicing in the fact that she knew exactly what she would be seeing after her battle with cancer was over.

Chapter 7-10 describes the sound of death, including a graphic description of hell and including the olfactory addition of burning flesh. Also, the whoosh – the audible exit of some.

Others include scenes from philharmonic vibrato and angelic throngs to a glowing rendition of a national intercessory prayer. The final story about the sound of death outlines an amazing gift of a love story of assurance in the ringing of a doorbell. Prepare to be mesmerized (this story was published in a national nursing journal).

Chapter 11 examines the smell of death, with a memorial tribute to those who have lost that sense, as their body is now in decay, either on a battlefield or in an intensive care bed. This is a particularly tender sense because it will often include the taste of death and decay, as well as the smell. It conjures up many sensibilities for those who have had relatives die of wounds and lethal damage from wars, revolutions, trauma, bombings, or gun violence. Imagine those precious young souls who died in the mud and gore in previous wars and religious conflicts. They haunt me and ask me to remember their sacrifice for freedom to worship and to believe in a hereafter.

Chapter 12 examines the sense of awareness. This story is extremely personal, as it tells the tale of the end of my loving husband's life. It examines his final gift of love to me, as his spirit floated over to me in a globe of light, touched me, and then exited. This was Jim's final reminder to share the reassurance and awareness that the spirit lives on and is like a light to overcome our fear. It was like my first extrasensory encounter with my grandfather, when I was three years old, recounted in chapter 3.

Proprioception is how your brain understands where your body is in space. This is why drivers who are pulled over and suspected of being impaired are asked to close their eyes and touch their nose. This sense is shared in chapters 10 and 11.

Chapter 13 is an invitation to tell your own story; ask your loved ones to share their stories while they are here. Ask them about their memories of their journey with you and record them so you can look back on them one day and laugh at the wonderful reality they shared with you. Don't wait until it's too late to ask them anymore, and you have to wonder what they were thinking.

Chapter 14 outlines some of the legal and ethical options available to people at the end of life. There's information on Medical Assistance in Dying (MAID), the merits of proper palliative care, and finally, burial options.

I want readers to explore their stories and be aware that death is simply a momentary transition of your soul to another state of consciousness. Your body takes one second to stop living, but I hope you will remember the miracles from the stories of these individuals in their journey from the end of one life to the beginning of another.

You pass through a veil of life to a glorious state of unconditional love and acceptance.

Your greeting as you arrive?

"Hi, God. I'm home. Wow!"

With love and gratitude that my wings are on.

1

The Invitation

TAP! TAP!

It taps on my heart.

"Are you there yet?"

Yes, I am.

For many years, I have wanted to share the exceptional flashes of revelation around death that I have been witness to. Yes, I've seen joy and peace around the final moments of a life.

Now is the time to share these stories.

I thought they were just incidents that happened to everyone, so I rarely shared them. You know, the kind you bookmark in your mind but you recount on rare occasions, as your intuition has deemed these stories important enough to pass along and assist others going through their experiences.

They remain in your mind like files that you keep, in case, and pages that you carefully turn down in a book so you can go back and read them again. They remain there inert because you are so busy, just paying your bills and meeting deadlines.

However, in the last decade, there has been such an unfolding to the awareness of the fact that we all die. This awareness has been accompanied by the question of, did we live our life's purpose? Did we in fact live out our life mission? Did we even know what it was?

Many boomers and zoomers have been able to avoid this reality; they live in a time of relative affluence and rapid expansion of technology. We live at such an accelerated pace that we cannot confront the planning of our funeral or even talk about our death (the only inevitability in life we all will accomplish). Doesn't it seem absurd that we would think there is no reason for being here? Why would God bother?

Why would we exist at all? Well, we are here to learn, and as many ancient philosophers and present-day gurus state, we are all spirits on a physical journey. I have always believed it most likely.

> For two thousand years, we have had this Bible promise: "For God so loved the world that He gave His only begotten Son, that whoever believes in Him should not perish but have everlasting life" (John 3:16 NKJV).

He even rose from the dead to show the way and add the exclamation point of eternal life.

Now I must share.

I am compelled to reassure, to give comfort, and to make easier our use of these words: death, dying, and the end of this life.

I have been part of many end-of-life scenarios, and my hope is that as I share some of them, you will be aware of those you may witness and share them with others to overcome our incessant fear of death and the unknown. Sharing with one another is essential and proven to be most therapeutic.

Death has no sting when we do not fear it.

> Oh death where is your victory; Oh, death where is your sting? (1 Corinthians 15:15–16 NKJV)

I spent over fifty years as a health care professional, with diplomas as a nurse, energy healer, naturopath, and bereavement counsellor; now, as a widow, the more that I have seen death, the greater I sense it is a passage. Your learning journey is over for now. You are graduating to a new reality. Is it birth to birth? Death is just that moment where we are released to transcend.

Yes, like a real birthday gift. These words may make you say, "Hush up. How absurd is that?"

The imperative part of the spotlight on that word *death* is that it emphasizes the importance of living your life with verve and inspiration because there is an end to this specific contract of time, known as your life.

But that is how great aha moments are incubated. It is called the collective consciousness. Like a long-nurtured birth of an idea, it takes many input neurons to build that awareness to a high enough collection of electrons to vibrate through the paradigm and turn an accepted idea on its head to examine the opposite conclusion. Maybe it is not an end but a beginning, another birth. Or is it more like the present theories that the initiation of a thought is a biochemical reaction formed before you really think it?

My intention is to invite you to be comfortable with death as the key to the next life, not a black abyss to be feared.

I share this book with you with Love and Light.

Put your angel wings on.

Wow. Come and sit with me for a while.

These are the stories that I have been given.

> *Watch. Stand fast in the faith, be brave, be strong. Let all that you do be done with love. (1 Corinthians 16:13 NKJV)*

2

The Grand Plan

FOR THE LAST fifty years, I have dealt intimately with death and life. I am a trained palliative care nurse. I have been at the bedside of more than thirty patients who died. Yes, right there. It was just timing. But you and I both know that synchronicity is usually just a part of your grand plan.

What do I mean by a grand plan? Did you ever feel like you were a pawn on a chess board? You are being directed by a grand idea that you consented to, and you are living out that plan. Did you ever look back and realize that what you thought was the worst thing that happened to you in fact turned out to be just another yield sign, stop sign, or even a sharp curve?

Did it in fact turn out to be the best thing because he was the wrong life partner or the job was not on your life plan and so it had to be gone? Was it your unconscious mind reminding you to return to your actual path?

Why do you choose to do what you do? Is it to heal you? Do we operate in a mirror dimension, where everything we do is to resolve what we invite into our consciousness?

Imagine a world where we took responsibility for what's happening to us in this moment. Imagine that we have invited this drama into our life to learn from it.

You can imagine the anger I provoke when I ask that question to someone who got into a hysterical rage over something someone did to them. They direct that anger at me because I dared to suggest that they had orchestrated it; they're mad at me because I dared to ask what part they contributed to the present drama.

What are they to learn from this situation? This thought is no longer too far out there.

It's not a new idea anymore. I had to look in that same mirror and confess a few for myself. I cannot take credit for this thought, but it has resonated with me for many years. On the side of my refrigerator is a tattered recipe card; you know, the kind that are held there by infamous fridge magnets and grow tattered after years of grease and smoke as we watch it get clearer in our mind. Thank you to Dr. Joan Borysenko.

"You are exactly where you are to be. You have chosen the scenario you are in, and you will remain there until you have learned your lesson/solution. I acknowledge where I am and who I am."

Yes, it becomes clearer. It has been there for forty years now. The first card blew away in a tornado; I found it on the ground in the pile of the rubble. But that story is for another day. How much like life that is; the more times we get burnt like the smudge over the recipe card, the clearer the message.

The sadder the experiences, the greater joy we feel.

The more we see pain and suffering, the more we feel driven to alleviate them.

The more we mourn, the more we rejoice when that gray numbness clears.

The darker our emotional state, the greater the contrast of delirious light.

The more we feel pain, the greater the joy when it's absent.

Finally, the more we see death, the more we appreciate life.

I used the following verse in the preface to my first book:

> *To everything there is a season, a time for every purpose under heaven. A time to be born and a time to die. (Ecclesiastes 3:1–2 NKJV)*

3

The Gift of Death: You Are Still Here, Babby

THE VISION OF SPIRIT

I FIRST REALIZED that people around you die when I was three. In those days, when you had recurrent tonsillitis, like I did, they were usually taken out. Mine were scheduled to be removed one day in the local hospital. The elective surgery was done, but they couldn't stop the bleeding, so I was sent to a large hospital in Toronto, about a hundred miles away. I remember my mother's beautiful black coat with the square collar trimmed with fur that she had on as she explained why I had to go. It was always such a clear imprinted memory. It was serious. I was so afraid of this unknown.

My first day at the hospital was busy: what to eat, how was I feeling? So many new faces. The menu was less than spectacular; poached egg on a white plate with a metallic clanging cover and a can of ginger ale and a glass of apple juice. I tried to swallow a sip of ginger ale, but it just would not go down, so it seemed like a fine idea to combine them all in a handy space left in the upper half of that juice glass.

Oh my, the nurse was not impressed. After that, the tray went clanging away. I rested for a while and then decided it was time to go home. From my spindled crib, I carefully pulled out the drawers of the metal nightstand into a descending set of steps, to arrange my escape. I piled the pillow and blanket high enough to get out over the crib side and carefully made my way down the steps of the nightstand. I went straight to wherever everyone else went to disappear from the place: the elevator.

I had seen it on my way up to the floor and saw that all you had to do was push a button to go up or down. I knew I had to go down because I was eight floors up in the air. I had never been in such a tall building, nor in an elevator, but it was the way out. I was sure.

As I stood at the elevator to await my exit, I had a problem: I could not reach the button, so I had to wait. A very tall man dressed in green scrubs and wavy white hair kindly asked me, "Where do you think you are going, young lady?"

I clearly replied that I was going home to see my Babby and Mommy and Daddy. Eventually, I was invited to take this kind man's hand, and he promptly accompanied me back to my room.

They did seem impressed with my escape route, though. I do remember the words "good planning." I remember now, but it didn't feel that way at the time. My parents did come later that afternoon, though, and the nurse told them the story.

The next day was another repeat of unattractive meals, and I tried the same charming combination of food, still not able to swallow, before it was hurriedly taken away. Next was a trip on a stretcher to the operating room, and I recall being very sleepy. As I awoke and looked out the tall windows into the cold February sky, the glowing sun looked cold and yellow. You know, the steely grey clouds and a shimmer of pale yellow as the sun sets. That was my view from eight stories off the ground.

I was whimpering, alone.

When I opened my eyes again, I saw my grandfather (I called him Babby), standing in that tall window. The sky was grey behind him, but a bright gold light seemed to be glowing all around him.

I could not talk, but I recall thinking to him, *Hi, Babby.*

His voice was clear, the tone familiar: "Don't worry, honey; you'll be okay. Look for the chocolate bar in my vest pocket."

I smiled. I was not alone, and then, he was gone. Where were my parents? I had seen my Babby; where were they? I closed my eyes again, and then it was morning.

The next day, when my parents came, I was so happy. We all hugged, but I felt my mother's tears on my face as she hugged me.

"What's wrong, Mommy?" I asked.

The reply came: "Well, honey, your grandpa went to heaven yesterday." Both Mommy and Daddy were crying. When my father got home from work the day before, he had found my grandfather on the ground at his car door in the snow; he had died on the way to see me.

I looked at my parents and said, "But he did; I saw him yesterday in that window right over there. He had a light all around him and told me where my chocolate bar was."

After that, I never had any doubt that our spirit is released from the shell of our body and goes on. No, never.

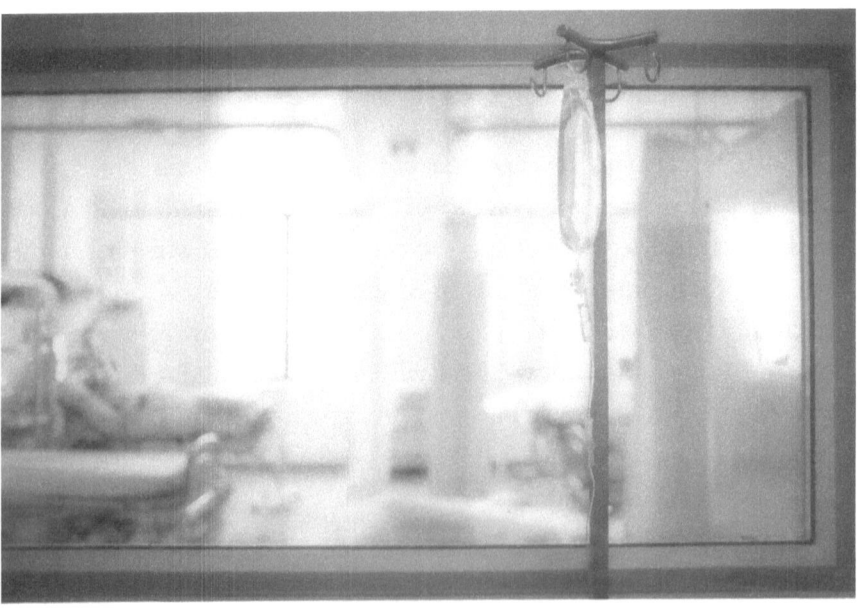

4

The Wisdom of the Farm

BEING RAISED ON a farm where there are animals is another great lesson of the reality of death. Years ago, you might have counted twenty cats around the barn, and then suddenly, there were only two. This was all part of the cycle of life because they took care of the mice and rats that ate holes in the bags of feed, causing waste and being a real nuisance. You become very accustomed to the phrase, "Oh, a few died; likely distemper." It was the balance of nature on a farm.

Another lesson is my answer to a question that's often asked in casual conversation: "Did you ever have a dog?"

I would jokingly answer, "Well, more like disposable dogs."

I imagine it sounds so flippant, but it was true. We lived on a busy second-line road, and dogs were not tied up or confined. Dogs lived a great life; they were free to roam the fields, hunting down groundhogs, hopping through fields of mustard and grain, pursuing a visiting cat, and merrily following the tractor and equipment up and down the rows. Haying was the best sport because the moles would be exposed under the hay windrows and be fair game for a game of chase and catch again or sometimes gotcha.

Yes, they would die, but the balance of nature was assured. Every animal had a purpose. Everything lived for a while but eventually died.

Some animals had to die so that we and others could eat. It was the cycle of life on the farm. All things had a purpose.

Sadly, too many of our dogs would naively follow the equipment, oblivious to the danger, and be hit on the road. They would then become another name on the disposable dog list. Each one was a sad event. Each one would cause a time of grief with storytelling of their habits, their personality, and finally their demise. Just for the record, I recall there being nine dogs in my seventeen years on the farm. when I moved to Toronto to train as a nurse, working in emergency, I remember thinking that the statistics on people were much higher. We would maybe see that in a week. What a lesson.

I remember thinking (well, at least with animals), if they were sick and withering with pain and no hope of getting better, we could put them out of their misery. It was a sad and difficult task for my father, but even as a child, you could feel the animal's sense of relief.

Dying was a sense of relief and release for the suffering animal. No more pain.

During those youthful years, older relatives and neighbors would die, but they were surrounded with muted comments such as "Well, she lived a full life" or "What a peaceful way to go," even if a tractor had rolled over on them or they had gotten caught in the forage harvester and it was instantaneous. That one was met with the saying "Well, at least he did not suffer long."

Of course, one of the most important foundational aspects of my belief of the inevitability of death and the assumption that it was not permanent, was the gift of being completely immersed in a Christian home and environment.

There was no swearing. There was no shopping on Sundays. There was always church on Sunday at 10 a.m., Sunday school following, choir practice Thursday night, and church euchre or social one Friday night a month. The special entertainment times with the community were church dinners and chicken barbeques in the parking lot of our humble country church.

We had an incredibly special task: boarding the minister's cats when he went into the mission field. The only Sunday we took off was in August, when the minister was on holiday and we went to Wasaga Beach to get a total sunburn and play in the water. Other times, we would play in the local river after a hot day of loading hay or shoveling grain into the granary.

The acceptance of faith was lived wholly by my family. The trust in God was especially palpable when there was a crop failure and the yearly potential ended up being a very smelly pile of fermenting turnips, instead of a newer car that started every time.

It's not that we were different from any others on Erin Township's second road. We just didn't know that we were poor. We were all relatively the same. We had a wonderful gift: faith that we would always have enough food and that God would take care of us. It was in the Bible.

We were raised on simple songs, like "God sees the little sparrow fall; it meets His tender view. If God so loves the little bird, I know He loves me too" and "Yea, thou I walk through the valley of the shadow of death, Thou art with me, thy rod and thy staff, they comfort me."

The wind in the maples for me was like singing "Breathe on me breath of God, fill me with life anew."

We also understood that Jesus was always there. We could pray to him any time for anything. He was our friend. We just had to obey the rules, and there were only ten, with a few additions like, "Love thy neighbor as thyself" and "Take time to listen" and "Be kind." These were the rules of our home.

Papa often hired people who needed a hand up, including slow learners and local boys who had just gotten released from the reformatory. We had not heard of ADD or ADHD yet. Papa knew they needed money for food. Mom would bake pies for every one of our church dinners and never missed giving food to people who had a death or illness in their family. Those were the rules of a Christian spirit.

Of course, the core message was that if you obeyed the rules, you would go to heaven, and that was the most important goal. It was to have eternal life; yes, eternal life. We learned very clearly that God had sent his Son to the earth to forgive us our sins, as we forgive those who sinned against us. These were the solid rules of life. Most importantly, though, was the fact that even when Jesus was hung on the cross to pay for our silly human gang (that's how I refer to us), He rose from the dead on the third day. There was always this guidance: If you died, you did not stay there but went to heaven, if you obeyed the rules, and to hell, if you broke one of the Ten Commandments. You could escape condemnation if you humbled yourself and asked for forgiveness and believed that He rose from the dead. That was the promise, and we never questioned it.

Our grandmother lived a life of humility and grace; she had a kind demeanor. She homesteaded in Saskatchewan and raised six beautiful, strong children with nothing but faith. But I never heard her complain, ever. Each morning, she would rise with a prayer and say another at her afternoon nap and another as she went to sleep.

We saw our courageous mother sing "How Great Thou Art" and "The Lord's Prayer" in her beautiful operatic voice at every local wedding or funeral. And our father was always optimistic and determined, with a consistent faith. Any large problem? Just get on your knees behind the barn and pray.

Yes, humbly pray.

This was the wonderful, enduring faith that was the foundation of my soul and belief. I always believed that death was simply the key to heaven, after we had done our job as assigned. What a gift to give to everyone. We are loved. We are God's children, and he has a place prepared for us when we die. The promise was clear. He had sacrificed his Son so that we could have everlasting life. "For God so loved the world that He gave His only begotten Son that whoever believes in Him should not perish but have everlasting Life" (John 3:16 NKJV).

As I headed to Toronto, at the age of seventeen, there was never any question in my mind. In fact, eventually, you hear the rest of the promise. You are already saved by grace. We just must accept the invitation and live it.

> For by grace have you been saved through faith, and that not of yourselves. It is the gift of God. (Ephesians 2:8 NKJV)

5

Wisdom of the Children

THE ONLY EXCEPTION to an orderly scheme of life was the first time I saw a child's tiny white casket being brought into our lovely rural church for a funeral. The comments around this situation were much more laden with pain and tears.

The question was there: Why would a baby die in a crib? Any explanation was hollow and full of fear and pain. It pointed out the randomness of life, which was no real answer. It did point out, though, the finality of death. People who have died are gone and disappear from this plane of reality. We would not see this being again.

My other recollection was of Robbie, a sweet boy with amazing eyes (one was blue and one brown). He often came to our home and played with our cousins and our family pod of four kids. He was a fun, laughing spirit and a bit of a mutt. My fondest memory of him was when we were given a real treat one Saturday afternoon in the parlor.

First, it was unusual to eat in the parlor, which was generally reserved for ladies and their china teacups, but not for kids or their food. But this day, Mother relented and served us a real treat. She did not purchase baked goods often but had gone to the A&P and found the piece de resistance: sultana spice cake. They were filled with the largest raisins I had ever seen and were truly a delicacy. As we salivated over this treat, I noticed Robbie was curling his lip at these strange fruits and rolling one around in his mouth. I then looked after my little sister and carried on.

Nothing more was said, but about an hour, after Robbie had left, my mother looked up on the eight-foot-high ceilings, and there they were: three globs of sultana raisins, glued to the plaster swirls. Oh my. That is the mutt part. The reason this memory is so imprinted is that we never saw Robbie alive again. About a month later, we heard that he had died of appendicitis.

Death just meant absence. Again, the remarks around that death were muted and sad; the question again was raised: Why did he die so young? It felt out of order. The only thing that remains is the memory of that spark of energy, that sparkle of laughter and joy. We remember the delightful mischief of a sweet spirit. We retold this story many times. Is it with the same delight that we secretly wish we could be free enough to do the same when something doesn't taste good? It is so much more comforting to believe that his spirit goes on.

There are many stories of people who know they have had a visit from a loved one who has passed away. For centuries, books have been written and tales told by talented storytellers.

6

When is Someone Dead?

MY NEXT GEM of wisdom was when I was assigned for my pediatric rotation to the same hospital in Toronto where I had been sent when I was three years old to stop my tonsils from hemorrhaging. This provided me with four very profound insights.

(Note: Fifteen years earlier, I met a tall man at the elevator; I met him again as I was heading up to Neonatal Intensive Care. He was now head of pediatrics. I could never forget that voice and face.)

The first observation was seeing a baby who appeared normal in size and weight but was born with no brain. "Anencephalic" is the medical term, which covers the clinical aspect, but what about the emotional?

How does one rationalize this decision? Ethically, we are bound to preserve and nurture life, but what about function? The anguish of the parents and the specialists, from pediatricians to neurologists to clergy; what is the right thing to do? It was the topic of several grand rounds and an opportunity to observe the true dilemma that faces those caring professionals in the question of "When are we alive?"

In my humble opinion, it was back to my primary response: How was it ethically or morally correct to have to wait until a massive infection finally brought this peripheral suffering to an end (peripheral in the sense that the mother and father that had to bear witness to the decline to death)? To an observer, the involuntary twitching and shudders of autonomic neurological response were impossible to watch, but did this wee being feel it or acknowledge it without a brain?

There is an awareness that this is the extreme, but it does happen.

It brings us to a new level of thought and examination of the definition of quality of life. Would a lethal injection be the only humane end gift to this unfortunate anomaly? I don't know. Do you?

PRECIOUS ZARA

The second observation was an eighteen-month-old girl brought in with convulsions. This fragile darling was admitted to Emergency by a frantic young mother covered in tattoos, fully drug-induced dilated pupils, and a questionable explanation of the history of how it happened. At that time, forty years ago, suspicions of child abuse could only be raised if there was a witness. That night on admission, there was a wonderful, sensitive third-year resident on call. Dr. Rob had an intuitive sense of what was going on with his tiny patients. He had a true gift of being able to see and feel the truth for these little ones who could not speak for themselves. He immediately ordered full-body X-rays. The results showed over twelve visible factures on the wee girl's frame. Some aged, some new.

We all were horrified.

During the six hours after the wee one was admitted, her level of consciousness declined. She already had one pupil dilated and fixed. Head injury was now on the list. While awaiting the results of the EEG, there was a final convulsion. All attempts were made to alleviate any further pain; CPR did not bring her back. No one spoke, but certainly my thoughts cried out, *Thank heaven, this little one can be released from inhumane suffering.* The relief of death was a gift.

Sadly, nothing could be done to bring forward charges for an obvious case of prolonged abuse until legislation was changed to get intervention and get help for these unnurturing mothers.

It stays in your soul though, like an echo waiting to be heard.

PENELOPE: CATALYST OF CHANGE

About two weeks later, I had the privilege of working with this same senior resident. Dr. Rob had just admitted a two-year-old with a facial laceration, which looked much like a hair lip abnormality, but the cut on the flesh was fresh, not healed and rolled, as it is with a hair lip defect. Obviously, someone had taken scissors and cut open a hole for the bottle. The mother was reported to have been screaming, "But she was going to starve if she didn't drink. She was going to starve." But again, without witnesses, you could not lay charges.

It was hard to avoid being critical as I took the child up to her room three hours later, following some initial care in preparation for eventual plastic surgery. I held her and walked her for several minutes to give her energy and love, as all nurses would.

I just happened to be the witness in another lesson that I had to learn. The mother came up to the floor; when she saw me, she said, "You better take good care of my Penelope."

I must admit that I was not as enlightened then as I am now, so many lessons later; instead, I replied, "Oh, lady, if I had my way, you would never touch this child again." Not the best protocol but my rage was on high for the obvious abuse and the frustration of not being able to prove anything because, again, we had no witnesses.

As a result of this case, Dr. Rob started a petition to change the legislation to be able to bring forward charges where there was irrefutable evidence of abuse. We helped with the petition, but this truly impassioned doctor drove the legislative change. It took six months to organize.

Two months later, Dr. Rob, this angel of change, died of acute leukemia. It seemed that his mission was complete, his life purpose fulfilled. His death was a sacrifice to push the legislation through with great speed. His quote to us was, "Don't worry; my purpose must have been to do this, and now I am going home." Wow.

Once again, the death was the gift. There have been many more examples of early death driving a cause. I am sure you know of some yourself. This was my first.

> Out of the mouths of babes and infants You have ordained strength, because of your enemies, That You may silence the enemy and the avenger. (Psalm 8:2 NKJV)

ANGELA'S GIFT

The final example occurred after Dr. Rob died; I was having a difficult time dealing with his death, with the ugly face of child abuse, with the irreconcilable question with no answer: why were they born if they only lived a short time? Why all the pain? Why all the anguish? Where was God?

I went so far as to write a paper on the theory that there should be universal birth control and people would have to apply for the antidote and get a permit to prove they had enough love, energy, and will to raise a child.

I almost got expelled for that one. But another lesson and answer would come.

As part of my clinical experience at this world-class pediatric hospital, I worked with newborns up to age five, and then we switched and I covered six up to sixteen years old.

The first day I walked onto the six- to sixteen-year-old floor, I was greeted by a beautiful girl with curly blonde hairs and bright blue eyes. She was looking over the six new nursing students who were walking onto the floor, where they would work for the next six weeks. She was interviewing each of us as we passed her while standing there with her IV pole of courage, like a sweet angelic warrior.

Finally, it was my turn to be scrutinized. She looked up at me with a gleaming smile, an aura of energy around her, and beautiful smoky blue eyes. Her skin was already waxy in color, her eyes already sunken into their sockets, her head bare after years of chemo, and the veins clearly visible through that opaque skin. She said, "Hi, you must be my new nurse. I am Angela. I am going to be an angel soon."

Here was my lesson: so calm, so forthright, so sure, so happy, so faithful in her awareness. *Thank you, thank you, sweet spirit*, I thought, as a tear rolled down. Again, death was her gift of complete faith.

She knew she was going on to be an angel with that wonderful innocence of a knowing spirit. Wise, so wise in a six-year-old girl, but her mission was accomplished. Angela taught us all. She had knowledge beyond us. She was calm, no fear, no question. Just knowing.

7

The Sound of Death: Whoosh

MY NEXT WONDERFUL lesson was from a dear eighty-five-year-old man. I will call him Mr. Tony. Mr. Tony was a sweet Portuguese man. He loved to talk of his favorite foods, especially baklava, his family, and Maria, his dear wife, who had already died a year ahead of him.

Most medical students worked night and afternoon shifts. They were wonderful learning opportunities; we made independent decisions and trained in management. The other amazing part was the real talks you could have with your patients. They wanted to talk about their lives, but even better was when they wanted to share the wisdom they acquired over the years. They shared their important lessons with their families and even the young nurses.

They had lived.

They had seen war. They had seen revolution. They knew deprivation and real loss.

They knew they were dying and soon.

Mr. Tony's family had been given the news of his terminal diagnosis. The order on the paper chart (yes, paper) was that we were not to discuss this with him. We were forbidden, by the family. The order was written in red marker.

So the parade of visitors began to Mr. Tony. You know, the muted voices, the pretend laughter, the mundane conversations that happen when the family is not comfortable with the thought that Dad, Grandpa, Uncle, or friend, that Mr. Tony is dying and soon.

Sometimes, there's a major drama as the family jockeys for position of who will get the most, who deserves the most. Family feuds become exaggerated as the fear of loss starts to sink in. There is even the positioning for who will be there to have the bragging rights that they were there for the last breath. It is like watching people plan a trophy hunt.

Grieving has already started. They just don't know that they are in between shock and denial and anger.

For four days, Mr. Tony's parade was very busy. I was on day shift, and there were a few skirmishes because on a public floor, with eight patients in an open public unit, with only curtains separating each patient, visitors were restricted to two at a time. Others were relegated to waiting in the hall by the elevator.

I went back on nights. On my second night, Mr. Tony asked if we could please talk, when I had a moment. About 2 a.m., after I finished rounds and meds for the forty-two patients on my floor, I came to visit with Mr. Tony. I stood at his bedside, held his hand, and said, "Hi; what do you wish to talk about?"

Another wow moment: He asked me outright, "I am going to die, aren't I? How can I let my family know that it is okay? I have made peace with my God. I know that I am going to my heavenly home. I want to tell them that I am ready and have no fear. I want to tell them that their mother is waiting for me. She has come to visit me in my dreams, and she is waiting. I know that my family has told you not to tell me, but I want them to know that I know. I am dying, right?"

I nodded my head.

How can you not acknowledge their wisdom? How can you not tell the truth? They know already. He just grabbed my hand and kissed it and thanked me.

"*Gracia, gracia,*" he said, laughing. Soon, he could go home to be with his Maria.

So we talked.

"What did your Maria say?"

"Oh, it is so beautiful there. All my family is there waiting for me. I have seen the Praia de Arrifana Portugal. I have flown over it just last night, but I had to come back."

Innocently, I had no idea what the Algarve was, but he described it so clearly. Rocky cliffs, aqua green foaming waves, and warm, warm winds to float him there. So he spoke with a gleam of youth in his eyes and a light of spirit as he described his beautiful place of birth. He had never actually seen it himself in this life, but he had already envisioned his destination and beyond.

He then stated, "I will tell them tomorrow, yes? I want to tell them the truth."

"Yes," I said. "If that is what you wish, then you must. They will know your peace of exiting this life. It will be a great assurance to them eventually."

He then closed his eyes and slept for the rest of the shift.

When I came in for 11 p.m. the next night, I was told to talk to the head nurse the next morning. Miss Roma told me the family was angry that I had discussed his death with him; I was given the typical message of "It's not your job."

I nodded but smiled as I walked away.

Mr. Tony was ready. I walked down the corridor towards the elevator. Just as I went to push the button, a small voice spoke in my head and said, "Go to Mr. Tony now." I returned to his bedside. I pulled the curtain around and looked. At that second, I heard the most amazing whoosh, and it ascended upwards from Mr. Tony's body. He took his final breath and was gone. His spirit had lifted from his now limp body.

Wow. Thank you, Mr. Tony; you gave me the gift of the sound of death.

Poof; we are gone.

He was free and home with his Maria and his God. I recalled the following verse:

> *But those that wait upon the Lord shall renew their strength;*
> *They shall rise up with wings like eagles. (Isaiah 40:31 NKJV)*

8

Visions of Death

"NO. I DON'T WANT TO BE HERE!"

FOR THIS STORY, I must make a confession. I've read several books about other people's stories of death and heard many patients speak about their life journeys, and I started to question if there really was a hell. Several of these books explored the following principles:

- Light is not possible until you see the contrast with darkness.
- Joy is not nearly so delicious until you experience the depths of sadness.
- Love is so divine when you realize the desert of apathy.
- Yin is not discernable unless you know the yang.

I started to believe in reincarnation, which posits there is no hell. I wrote these questions in my journal to ponder as I read these best sellers. I started to question the principle of how a God of love could banish you to such a place as hell, even though it was indoctrinated in all my early discipline and Sunday school stories.

How was it possible?

Mr. Carlos was a seventy-year-old gentleman in his final stages of cirrhosis. In his case, the liver was irretrievably damaged after a lifetime as a brittle alcoholic.

Alcoholism is a disease. It seems similar to a diabetic who cannot live without the fix of sugar, but society is often judgmental when the diagnosis is alcoholism. I am not. It has always seemed to me to be the harshest addiction; why would you ever choose to imbibe that which is killing you?

Alcoholism destroys the person afflicted and so much more. Carlos had lost all his family; his wife and two daughters left. They had been gone from his life for over ten years. They could not help him love himself or them more than he loved the bottle. He lived alone in a small town in our area. He had no one to call on him or visit. He was dying alone.

Our treatment team cared for him and managed his pain; we could see the final toll of liquor addiction; he was unable to tolerate food or liquid. So sad, so alone, so much self-loathing, so many regrets.

One day, though, as I went in to do an assessment, I was greeted at the door by a lady about his age. She said she was his ex-wife and explained that she could not see him die alone.

Another lesson: Love never dies; sometimes, it just hurts so much that you must leave to save yourself. She had done this. Her simple touch comforted him; she willingly bathed him and managed his pain as he shrunk daily into the skeleton that held his spirit.

They talked. They healed.

They forgave one another.

One day, he lost consciousness.

Finally, one afternoon, I was doing my final check; he was now in the final stages of death. His wife asked me to call their daughters; she took the phone and spoke these words: "Can you come? Your father is dying. Just come and say goodbye."

His breathing was shallow, his pupils were fixed, and he was unresponsive to any stimuli. No urinary output; we just kept him comfortable with enough pain meds to alleviate any further suffering.

The girls agreed to come and say goodbye. They had forgiven him also. We all know how important this step of forgiveness is; it benefits the forgiver.

I checked in about 7 p.m. on my way home for dinner and reassured his wife that if he were to die in the night, I was on pager and would come and do the pronouncement. All things were in place; the funeral home, the plans, and the girls, we hoped, would arrive in time.

Families are offered the option to stay with patients for a while, and then we will come. It is up to them; they just record the time of passing since it is an "Expected Death in the Home" (EDITH).

(Note: EDITH is the comical acronym nurses often used to discuss the elephant in the room, when we avoid talking about death, dying, and planning for the obvious reasons.)

That night, I kept one ear open, waiting to hear the pager alert me that he was gone and deceased. I woke at 6 a.m., after two hours of peaceful sleep. I jumped into my uniform and headed to their home, about five minutes away, and knocked on their door.

When I walked in, there was Carlos, sitting on the edge of his bed. How was this possible? I looked at his wife, who was standing there at the kitchen door with tears running down her cheeks.

Eyes wide open, in shock, I gasped and finally said, "Wow. Carlos, what happened?"

"Oh, Bev," he said, "where I was going, it was so hot, so hot. People were screaming so loud, so many, so loud. They were crying and screaming, crying and screaming. I yelled out, 'No, I don't want to be here; no. No! Let me go back! Let me go back and make it right.' I was so hot, and the screams grew louder and louder from those that were in the raging fire. I could smell their burning flesh."

Carlos could feel an omnipresence of light; he had been given an opportunity to press the correction button on the brokenness in his life.

"I pleaded, 'Let me go back,' and I whooshed back. Awake! I am here to make it right," he said with tears in his eyes.

"Wow," I exclaimed. "Thank you, Lord" (I could not hold it back). They repeated the same prayer.

They requested that I call the girls and explain that their father was not dead, that he had come back and wanted to talk to them. I gently thanked Carlos for teaching me this lesson and allowing me to witness this miracle, this story of redemption and forgiveness.

For the next three weeks, they all communicated: they cried; they laughed; they emptied anger out and let the light of love in.

One morning, he was found in bed, dead. His purpose was fulfilled; the story that had unfolded was amazing (which seems like such an inadequate word for this situation). I retell this story many times to teach reassurance and redemption.

Thank you, Carlos. Your lesson to us? Be aware there may be a hell, so keep living by the rules.

- Love one another as I have loved you.
- Love yourself as I have always loved you.
- Fear not; I am with you always.
- Know that I am.

THE PROFESSOR'S REVELATION

The professor had been the head of a department at the University of Toronto. He was a tall, wise soul. He was classic in his appearance, with wavy white hair and clear blue eyes, but the smoke ring of death was around those gray-blue irises. He had end stage Hodgkin's and was dying.

I had visited four or five times that month, and each time, he wanted to engage in a stimulating conversation of why he was a confirmed agnostic. We would banter, and because I always retorted that it was not possible to argue about something that didn't exist, he would smile.

"In truth," I'd say, "God just might be real if it took that much energy to argue that he does not exist."

He would laugh, and he always chuckled when I ended my visit with my exit phrase, "Well, take care, and keep your wings on."

I had heard a report and knew that his energy was depleting rapidly; the end of his life was coming shortly. He was bedridden all the time now and taking in minimal food or liquid. He was dying soon, and he knew it.

When I walked in that final day, his daughter greeted me with the following statement: "Well, they are all around him."

She wondered if I was open to such a dialogue, and I was. She told me that the room was full of multiple spirits on all sides of the room and close to the ceiling of the eight-foot-high walls of their lovely Victorian home.

Prof lay there, calm and peaceful, his beautiful brown Lab lying next to him. He replied yes for comfort and no pain. I completed the perfunctory measurements of his pulse and blood pressure, and chatted about how his family had come home to be with him. They had all arrived in within the last week and shared a wonderful reunion. The son lived in Malaysia, working at the university where his father had done research. One daughter, a physician, lived in Switzerland, and the other daughter was a pediatrician in California. Their spouses stood in the back of the room for support.

Their mother, his wife, had already predeceased him. They had had a lovely marriage, and he had told stories about her with a gentle smile, sharing warm tales of family trips around the globe, in particular, an excursion to ancestral Scotland, from where his forebears emigrated to Canada. What a wonderful legacy; his three children had arrived from across the world to bid him farewell. One of the daughters was aware of the spirits in the room; she was alone in her belief, but she did not hold back.

They were here, at least twenty of them, she said.

Suddenly, the Prof woke up. His eyes were wide, and he had a visible smile across his face. They all moved in closer to their father and held hands around him, like the circle of awareness they had felt at their mother's death four years previously.

They stood vigil around their dad. The room was silent.

The dog looked up to the corner of the ceiling and stood up.

The Prof haltingly whispered the following: "Bev, you're right; listen to that music. It's the most amazing philharmonic orchestra I've ever heard; so many harps. Listen to that choir; there are hundreds of them.

All shining white, all so bright. They are angels. There are so many harps, violins, angels. Thousands! Oh, my; hi, darling. Hi, Mother. Hi, Dad. Hi, brother. They are here; they are all reaching out to me."

His face looked illuminated. Not a wrinkle, not a concern. "They are inviting me home."

Measured, joyous words.

He reached his hand up to the corner, and then it dropped.

His spirit was gone; he was home.

The dog kept looking up and then gave a short bark.

I choose to believe it was "Goodbye."

Wow, what a revelation.

He had his wings on and had flown home.

May God be with him.

9

The Nationwide Prayer

ANOTHER MIRACLE STORY is that of the head priest of one of the largest churches in the world. This gentleman, who was almost seven feet tall, had been diagnosed with acute leukemia and was admitted to our floor one Thursday afternoon.

He was tall, bald, and so massive in stature, but his diagnosis betrayed his physical presence. He even required an extra large sheet to wrap around his gown.

The admission proceeded as usual. He was most polite and remained full of energy, even though his blood work showed that his white blood cell count was at a dangerous level. The blood work was once again repeated, and all samples done in a routine admission.

After the paperwork was complete, a group of visitors from his head office entered the room and began taking copious notes. I left them in privacy. About an hour later, after they were gone and he had had a small rest, I returned to his room and greeted him with a respectful "Bless you." I then asked him the routine questions of how he was doing and feeling.

His reply still echoes in my heart:

"Now, Miss Nurse, don't you worry. I have all the temples [tabernacles] across North America praying for me. You watch; I will be tested Monday morning again. They will not believe the results, and so they will repeat them, and I will be discharged by Monday night. You will see the miracle of mass prayer."

I held those words in my heart and marvelled at his overwhelming strength and the genuine faith in his statement. I had heard of the power of prayer from the missionary couple whose cats we cared for when they went into the mission field in Africa. I had not yet experienced it for myself in my midtwenties, but in my heart, I did believe it was possible, if God wanted it to be so to complete a life purpose.

I was off Sunday and came back in on Monday at 4 p.m. for my evening shift.

I took report, but there was no mention of this man. I waited until we were finished with the other forty-one patients. Usually, if there's no mention of a name, it usually means the patient has been transferred or has died.

I asked.

"Oh, he is just waiting for them to pick him up."

At 6 p.m., he was discharged from the hospital with a perfect blood count.

I walked with him to the elevator.

Thank you; thank you. Without a doubt, it was like a living parable to his church, a miracle to encourage and restore your faith. He stayed well for three more years and then retired. I do not remember his name, but I thank him for his miracle teaching. He was a true example of this principle: "You can heal yourself as long as you have a promise from a much Higher Power than you," especially if you know your purpose is to teach and you then fulfill that purpose to the end.

THE CATALYST OF STORY

I write these stories as a catalyst to start conversations, especially around the deathbed. Talk to people. Let them tell you what they see and feel. There are so many more stories, but I ask you to allow others around you to repeat their stories. So many are about returning to their country of birth as they die. They will recount playing on the seashore in Holland with their baby sister. They speak of seeing their deceased relative in full form, always younger and intact, no evidence of their end body as they appeared on their deathbed. Some even recall traveling in time to meet a relative who died thirty years before, their favorite grandparent or their mother. So many vivid memories to recall and repeat.

Please take the time to be easy with the stories around dying.

10

The Final Goodbye Bell

ROSIE: FOR WHOM THE BELL RINGS

MANY OF THE journeys of the community nurse occur far from the secured areas of private homes or city apartments. They take place in isolated, rural sanctuary holdings where people sought refuge from droning traffic or electromagnetic pollution. They choose to live in the middle of nature, with the tall dense greenery of burgeoning spruce trees and prolific numbers of warbling birds. Mother Nature is their refuge and tranquility.

One of these such calls was Rosie, a ninety-four-year-old woman in the final part of Stage 4 lung cancer, becoming increasingly short of breath and life energy. Again, a reminder that it is not just the body that dies and withers to the final stage of death; there are, in fact, two other components that comprise the exit of death. She was married; her husband was named Joe.

These three components are body, spirit, and soul. It is our body that erodes. Yes, it wears out.

It erodes with time, getting rusty due to things like arthritis. The air filter may get clogged, like in COPD, emphysema, and fibrosis. The plumbing starts to clog, get calcified, and decrease volume flow; it's called kidney stones, or benign hypertrophic prostate, where a gland becomes enlarged and impedes the urinary flow.

The result of this decline is often an increase in awareness of soul, as it starts to hear and feel more spiritual connections. The body allows you to go into low gear or even park, and you can see and feel what is around you.

You see the messages. You feel the awakening of your spirit; you become so much more mindful. How ironic it is that the quieter you become, the more definite and stronger the messages are to your spirit.

Rosie was now hearing more and feeling more as her body declined. She was one of the first patients to undergo radiation for the treatment of breast cancer. Physicians and radiologists knew that with radiation, the cancer cells appeared to be completely obliterated. It was finally felt that there was, in fact, a cure for those few cells that were still rogue in the patient's body.

Rosie had been asked to take part in some of the first human trials of radiation therapy, and she had consented. She told me this prior to my listening to her chest sounds with my stethoscope.

Oh, my; she was shy and embarrassed. I listened and tenderly reassured her. This was a trauma of an injury over sixty years old. Much compassion was required. I prayed silently for strength to show no negative emotions, no slight recoil of revulsion that could in any way add on to what Rosie had experienced for years.

"Bless you," I said.

I asked her gently to undo her blouse so I could listen clearly. I gave her all the control. She opened her shirt, and there was evidence of almost 80 percent scar surface across her chest and two large scars where her breasts had been sixty years ago. I felt and exhibited no revulsion. Only another eroded body, but a huge spiritual pain from a precious, sweet woman who had been an experiment to teach and advance the art of proper radiation.

"Tell me all about it," I said, proceeding gently and slowly. "I want to hear it all. Where did you have it done? How long did it take to heal, how many treatments did you have, how did they protect the rest of you, how painful was it, how did you manage the pain, how did you deal with it? What did they learn from the study? How did they follow up with you?"

She slowly addressed each question, and her answers grew more emotional the longer she spoke. She replied with that faraway glance of reminiscence and release that often happens when you ask those questions that count, the questions that provoke precious memories of a previous decade, when youth was still there, and you can almost wrap the memory with a bow, with the perspective of age and closure in sight.

"Were you already married? How did Joe deal with it? Did you ever tell him what you felt?"

"No" was her answer. It hurt too much to tell him of her embarrassment. She always wore a T-shirt.

"How would it feel to tell him now?" I whispered. "Oh, so good," she whispered back. "But how?"

"You just did; you are all practiced, and just feel that relief."

She sighed with an impish smile. "Oh, yes, I just did, didn't I?" Again, the gift of our impending physical end: our ego erodes.

"We just want to get it off our chest": such a statement. We must be prepared to hear their truth, their pain, their anguish in carrying whatever they have chosen as their burden of shame.

Finally, the intimate moment of relinquishing and sharing from the soul.

She took my face in her hands and asked, "Will you pray with me for strength?"

We did. She wanted so much to give Joe this gift of clarity and, above all, thank him for never asking too much about it. She wanted to thank him for seeing her beautiful glowing spirit and her sparkling eyes and always her mutual love. There was still time.

These routine visits continued for about two weeks, with Rosie growing weaker and weaker. She could no longer sit up but very lucidly stated that she was being visited in her restful periods by her relatives: her mother, her sister, and light beings.

On a cold, clear, crisp February day, she said, "Do you have time to sit longer?"

I did.

She wanted to tell me that she believed it was almost her time to go. Many of us do not have this clarity, but some do.

She talked of how she had all her paperwork in order. She had contacted the funeral home and gotten it all paid. All the bank business was attended to, and she had had so many wonderful talks with her family members.

She had talked and revisited so many great memories with Joe. They had laughed over the crazy stories about how they only had ten dollars but drove to the courthouse with their friends and got married. Tin cans rattled on their old car. They had reviewed all the great snapshots of time past, when they were so young to now, their present state, when they prepared to be alone.

She asked me to pray with her, and we did. It was a prayer of thankfulness for such a full and busy life. Thankfulness that she had survived early cancer and experimental treatment. She would see her late son, who had died at twelve, and her wonderful parents, who had not survived the war and incarceration in Poland. Thankfulness for the respectful love she and Joe had. Finally, she requested God to keep Joe safe because it was now her time to cross over, as she said.

Her face was calm and almost totally free of any life wrinkles. She was serene. Hers was the face of love and grace, as I said, "Amen and thank you, thank you, thank you for our wonderful Rosie and her contributions of love and light to this world." We hugged, and I left after reassuring them that I would come and pronounce her departure, whenever or whatever day that might be. It was noon as I walked to my car through the glistening snow.

At 1 a.m., I got a page. I called in and heard Joe's message" "Beverly, Rosie's gone; please come."

Jim, my dear husband, stirred and said, "I'll drive you, Angel. It's 1 a.m. and 30 below. Please let me drive you."

I hugged him and said thank you.

Their home was twenty miles south and two miles off the main highway. It was a gorgeous drive, so quiet and reverent. You know those drives where the highway is like a silver ribbon of moonlight ahead of you, and it feels like you can turn off your headlights to keep the view pure.

The fresh six inches of snow was light and fluffy as we drove the truck into Joe and Rosie's driveway. I got out and marked my path in with snow indentations to my knees and lifting my heels in each tread. The full moon glistened; when I got to the door, I looked around. No wind, no breeze, just a magical night where it feels like the stars are suspended in an indigo sky. How magnificent, a true portal of a universe so vast and so still.

Joe's eyes met mine. We shared a look combining disbelief and reality. He smiled, "She did it her way, quietly and with grace, didn't she? She's in heaven now. She is home." I agreed.

"What time exactly, Joe?" I asked.

"It was 12:22 a.m.," he said. "I woke right up. I felt her go. Beverly, I know it. We had talked it over; she said she would go with a smile. I was there holding her hand in bed beside her. I felt her spirit go, almost heard it, I think."

How wonderful; after sixty-eight years, I believe the "two [had] become as one," if we allow it, and it is the right one.

"She had everything ready," he said. "She told me you two had talked and prayed for an easy exit. She got her prayer answered. I've loved her forever."

I turned and went into her bedroom to perform the procedures of pronouncement. After listening with my stethoscope and doing a visual appraisal, I returned to the dining room table and removed the death certificate from the brown envelope of legal papers for the doctor to sign.

Rosie had her birth certificate and social insurance card on the table. She was ready to exit. It was now 2:22 a.m.; we had finished the paperwork and were chatting. We placed a call to the funeral home.

Joe reminisced about her wonderful organizational abilities and shared precious stories of their mutual respect.

Yes, mutual respect, that most essential element of a relationship. True love is not possible without mutual respect.

He also said that she was now his angel to guide him through this life. I so agree; I had often heard this phrase when couples believe they were meant to journey together, the magic thought that they had been placed in one another's lives to live, love, and laugh.

How sacred.

As we finished the last signatures, the doorbell rang. "Bing-bong." It rang again.

Joe chuckled and said, "Oh, that's Rosie. She was the only one who could ring the doorbell. The only one."

Wow. What a gift.

He laughed and said with a tear and a smile, "She is just letting us know she is out there and fine. Thanks, Rosie." Wow. What a love.

We were finished.

I walked to the door and looked out at the snowy walk. There was only one set of footsteps, just mine of an hour ago. No wind, full moon, and glistening powder. Jim was still waiting patiently in the truck.

I looked at Joe and said, "Can I just try the doorbell?"

"Sure, go ahead," he said, chuckling; he knew what would happen. I tried the doorbell twice; no sound.

"Yes! Only Rosie could make it work. I told you." I turned to walk to the truck.

Thank you, Joe and Rosie; another reminder that love lives on. Joe knew it and had been reassured of it.

The ending of death was not permanent to this couple. They genuinely felt they would see one another again in heaven. They felt such peace around the word *death*. They were comfortable with dying. They were satisfied that they had discussed all aspects of what they had learned together, how they had loved to dance and loved the family meals; loved hiking and feeling nature and seeing its beauty; how they had escaped to this beautiful country, away from a dictatorship and despair due to greed and the love of money and power.

They had known a sacred love; yes, sacred.

11

The Smell of Death

ON A BEAUTIFUL clear July day, I was covering in emergency when Pete arrived. The ambulance attendants were so busy. This was the youngest victim of a turf war between two motorcycle gangs in the core of Toronto. He had been caught in the crossfire between rival gangs and had been hit full frontal abdomen as he tried to take cover down a balcony and fire escape.

The wounds from a shotgun are insidious. They do not make a full open wound but instead enter through the skin, leaving a small hole, and the extent of the blast is not evident until X-rays are done. The officers quickly gave the patient's medical history, as far as they knew it. Pete was sixteen years old, not part of any gang, a good kid, well liked; simply in the wrong place, wrong time.

Pete smiled up with that fragile look of a cornered baby fox that wonders, *What am I doing here?* I held his hand, and we began the journey to the edge of life.

"We need an X-ray and cross match, stat," the doctor ordered. Done. BP was stable for the moment. He was young. He had a chance. One of the gang members had been in the next ambulance, but he died a few minutes after arriving to the examining room. No chance, gone; head injury, full blast.

The X-ray was up on the screen: so many pellets, but all abdominal, none in the liver or spleen. No immediate hemorrhaging at present.

The surgeon consult barked, "Take him up to OR; I have a slot available."

Pete looked at me with those velvet, frightened eyes.

I grasped his hand and said, "They'll take good care of you, Pete. Hang in there. Angels be with you."

"Thanks," he whispered. "Pray for me." "I will." I did.

On my next shift, I was assigned to care for Pete as a special duty in the intensive care unit. He was getting stable now. Youth is such a great gift when you have a medical incident. All those precious organs and systems are new. They have the best chance of survival and recovery. Pete was no exception. The surgeon and team had worked over three hours, removing over fifty pellets, but they couldn't risk more time checking that they had retrieved them all and had to close up.

Pete was just coming to consciousness, and we talked while the pain med was keeping him comfortable and partially sedated. The body heals so much better when at rest and in a space of homeostasis. It had been shocked and invaded. Time to adjust and heal, was the message.

I had the next three days off, and when I returned to the ICU again, Pete asked me many questions; he wanted to know what happened, what had they done in surgery, what about the others, and finally, why me? Yes, why me? The proverbial question of everyone when faced with a life-altering situation. "Yes, why me, nurse?" Wow, what a question; I didn't know then, and I still don't, but it is what it is. We will know the answer eventually, but not on this plane; maybe all will be revealed when we die.

For me, I wondered the same, and I was not yet able to look back and find a partial answer.

I wasn't assigned to ICU for the next three weeks, but I often popped in to see Pete. He was always asleep; his stats showed he was periodically spiking a temperature, but the wounds were healing, and he was being moved to the step-down floor.

The next week, I got assigned to the ICU again. Pete was suddenly in peril. He felt an odd taste and smelled something wrong in his breath.

His abdomen started to swell rapidly, and his temperature began to spike: all morbid signs of infection. They started massive antibiotics; he seemed to be responding but was fragile.

I entered the unit. I could smell the odor of gangrene. It was there in his quadrant. He was restless and starting to be confused.

Nature is so kind; if we are fortunate, it starts to protect us from the pain and tries to conserve the energy to attempt to heal. It is as if our body closes ranks.

When I left, he was resting. One level down in consciousness, still responding, but protected from any excruciating pain. I left and reassured him I would be back later for the night shift.

I slept and prayed that he would be protected and pain free. I arrived on the unit at 11 p.m. He had awakened and asked if I was there yet. I went over to his bed and said, "Hi, Pete."

He blinked slightly and mouthed "Hi." He awoke further and asked if it was time for more pain meds. The antibiotics were not working; the gangrene was winning the battle. The pain was excruciating. I saw it in his beautiful brown eyes. They were fully dilated with the pain. "I need more, please." It was not time yet. I gave him some healing touch, a reassuring hand, and said, "Let's talk."

His questions were the same as six weeks ago: "Why me? I did not do anything; I was just getting out of the way. Who is this God? I heard about him when I was young. I had a visit last night from somebody in a white robe. He looked like an angel, I think."

"Yes," I said. "They will be there when you leave this plane."

I told him the story about my grandfather. I told him how his spirit had left his body and had come to visit me when I was just three years old. Maybe he could do great work after his separation from his body to another level up. Sometimes, we don't know where those words come from, but I thank God they do and at the right time. The message is like a download.

He talked about his life. He had helped care for his mom, who had been a brittle alcoholic; she died after he cared for her for the last five years. He had never known his father, just a faint memory of him when he was five or so. He had already lived through much drama and heartache.

He looked at me and said, "Maybe it will be easier now that I die. I know I am, you know. I know that I am going to die. Now, can you please help me with more pain meds, please, please, please?"

The sob of irretractable pain is so deep and so profound. I immediately went to the phone and put an urgent call in to the attending doctor. Pete had had the maximum dose of sedation that could be legally prescribed.

The doctor called back, and I presented the facts to him.

"Sorry," he said. "I cannot increase it. I will lose my license."

I hung up the phone slowly. This was years ago; I was so tempted but could not break the law and oath of ethics. I returned to Pete and heard his pleas.

The sun was just rising over Lake Ontario.

"Please take him," I prayed. I held his hand. "Do you believe that Jesus rose from the dead and will be there when you arrive?"

He accepted with a nod. The pain was so profound. His fingers gripped and indented into my hand. How was this right?

I prayed silently, but I knew Pete heard.

He looked up at the corner of the ICU unit. The monitor fluttered. The ECG was slowing. It flatlined. Thank you; it was over.

But I prayed that someday, we'd be allowed to treat other humans the way we do our animals, and I closed his eyes with a "Bless you, Pete. You are now pain free; you've got your wings on and are safe. Bless you."

The fragility of the body had won. The spirit lives on; it has answers to learn and memories to learn from. Bless you, Pete.

PS. If you've ever been at the bedside of someone suffering the horror of rampant gangrene or cancer, you know that look, the resolve of knowing that the gift of death is so near. Imagine soldiers wounded in war. Have we done enough for them? Have we learned the futility of conflict? Have we learned to love our neighbor as our self?

We are still so uncivilized.

We must hear their pain of anguish; prevent the pain. Exit with dignity.

Spread the language of positivity. Why spend so much money and focus on preparing for war? Why don't we spend equal time and vision on creating peace?

Pay honest money for honest work. Pay an honest percentage to those who contribute.

There is enough.

We are one body, just many cells that all need nutrients.

12

The Spirit Goes On;
We Are Light Bodies

THIS STORY IS very personal. It involves a man I have known for over forty-three years. Jim Wilkins was my friend and protector for all that time. When I was twenty-three, I was debating whether to continue my relationship with him or follow my career and head to a prestigious American hospital and train to be a doctor. It is so hard when your heart is challenged by love versus the intrigue of earning my dream of medicine.

I was working in the ER at a large Toronto hospital and heading out for the evening shift, starting at three o'clock. I lived in a seedier part of town; all the rest of my buddy nurses were married off. The tally was eight bridesmaid dresses and four guest soloist duties. And another ten with showers, dresses, and wedding gifts. There was not much left in the savings account.

I headed down the final steps of my upstairs apartment, locked the door behind me, and stepped out onto the sidewalk to hike it to the bus stop. As I checked for my token, I felt a man's arm hooking onto each side of me; two rather disheveled men were attached at the end of them.

"Hi, honey," they greeted me. "We're going for a ride." My heart flipped; show no fear.

Stand bold; breathe in.

This was mid-afternoon, on a side street, in Toronto; not good. I looked at them; all my cool had to rise.

"Look, guys, I am in my uniform; I am on my way to emergency; who is going to look after you?"

"Oh, honey, we are just going to the Brass Rail" (a notable bar with great music and fun). "We know you will love it there. Let's go."

They just kept walking me towards their van.

I kept talking: "Come on, guys; how much rye have you already had? You don't need too much more; why don't you let me go to work?"

They kept walking, but I just kept talking.

"Come on, guys, come on; I have to get there. If you run into trouble at the bar, you need me there, not here."

My heart was bursting; I was praying and asking for my guardian angels to get here soon.

I kept talking.

"Come on, guys; let me go. I will see you later. Come on, drop your arms. There's my bus."

I yelled, and I lurched. They dropped their arms, and I ran. I flailed my arms at the bus driver and kept racing straight ahead. The door opened. I hopped in and started to cry.

Thank you, Lord. Thank you, Lord.

I explained to the bus driver what had happened and sat down. There were no cell phones then, like now; you could have called 911, but my call was answered.

Thank you, angels. The driver stopped right at the hospital entry and let me out with a nod.

As I walked onto the ER floor, a page came across the loudspeaker: "Call for Beverly Bruce."

I was still so shaken, and then this page. I picked up the phone at the desk; it was Jim.

"Hi," he said. "Are you all right? I've just had the worst feeling; I had to call and make sure."

I started to cry again. "Yes, I am now. And yes, I will marry you."

I told him what happened and then reported in and worked a busy shift. Eight hours later, he was waiting for me to drive me home to my apartment. He had worked a full day and then drove two and a half hours to be there at the exit door. What a way to start a marriage.

Three months later, we said I do. How could I not? He felt me across hundreds of miles.

Thank you, universe.

For over forty years, we worked hard and contributed to our community. There were lots of board meetings, pioneering research, a tornado that took our dream home and barn, another tornado on the highway to Chicago that lifted our van and four other men off its wheels, a run at politics, and meeting many amazing people, from Raoul Castro to Julio Iglesias, Brian Mulroney, Pierre Trudeau, Oscar Peterson, John Wayne, Charlton Heston, Queen Elizabeth, Queen Mother, Princess Grace, and Deepak Chopra.

Sometimes it felt like the movie *Forrest Gump*; we were just humble country kids with a vision that took us on a few journeys. Thank you for such a life balance of work and interesting cameos. Wow. I am in awe.

Each of these individuals invited an awareness to the truth of life. We are all one; we are not separate. We are all integral parts of the matrix of life. Each one is a cell that is connected. We must remain connected. If not, we risk becoming rogue, malignant, and at risk of causing harm, by not remaining connected to a life force of light. No one is more; no one is less.

Is it possible that we invite these souls into our lives to learn this? Is it possible that we therefore see each one as important, equal, essential? I believe so, but just like this journey I've been led on, the message I've agreed to spread, each wonderful person is an essential living lesson with a genuine contribution to the lives of others.

Wow. How blessed when we know that everyone we meet was invited to join us to learn from us or with us. Is that the real meaning to "love thy neighbor" and "all men [and women] are created equal"; thank you.

Now that the players have been identified, I will set the scene:

It was May 18, 2014, and the past five years had been challenging for Jim. It had become increasingly apparent that this man who had traveled to over forty countries and states, remembered everyone's name, and could speak easily to hundreds of people now needed help getting dressed.

We were just walking away from the internment of my precious Dad, who was being laid to rest next to my mom, whom we buried the previous spring. There they were, together after sixty-seven years of marriage, side by side again. My father had suffered from dementia, and his forgetfulness had increased over the last year because his best prompter and "fill in the gaps" partner had died a year ahead of him.

He had missed my mother so much and often carried her photo under his arm as he wheeled around the retirement facility in Guelph. They took such good care of him. They could hoist him, lift him in and out of his chair, and care for him to maintain his dignity and safety.

It was early spring, and the wind was still cold as Brenda and I walked among the tombstones and grave markers in Erin Township, where they had farmed since 1948. I held Jim's hand and arm, and Brenda was on his other side. We were the three Musketeers, we would say, as she also had been left alone after thirty-three years of marriage.

As we sat in the warmth of the car, he looked at me and clearly said, "This is no way to live, is it?"

There was a tear in his eye, in that moment of lucidity that often comes with a Lewy body diagnosis. He knew that he did not know. Wow; what a finality of thought. All you want to do at that movement is hug and protect this precious soul you have loved and lived with, because you feel the slide. We drove home after the wonderful family meal, and you could feel his sadness. You know that they have seen themselves.

The previous week, Brenda and I had gone to visit four prospective nursing homes that had openings for Jim. It was becoming increasingly hard to manage him at home. Sadly, he was already more debilitated than many patients we saw on our visit. Greg and Adena, our daughter-in-law, were so supportive because I was still trying to work from home until December, when I took a leave of absence.

On several occasions over the winter, Jim had gone outside in -20 degree C weather in his shirt sleeves, looking for his car keys. He wanted to go home. "I have to get home," he would insist. On a couple of occasions, Greg had to come and persuade him to get back into the house, and he would reluctantly oblige.

If you are living this scene, it's essential to not take it personally. Jim really wanted to go home; I knew he meant heaven. Bless you, darling. I know. Most of the time, we created a scenario that would de-escalate his disorientation; we made it fun, but that's a story for another book.

On May 22, 2014, we had just gotten dinner ready together and were sitting at the kitchen island; he took my hand and said, "You know that cook thing?"

"You mean this meal?" I replied. "No; you know when you die?" "Oh, you mean cremation, honey?" "Yes, that. I don't want that."

"Oh; no problem. You want to be buried like Dad?" "Yes," he said, smiling.

"No problem. I will look after that, dear; we still have time. We'll go and pick out a plot instead of ashes on the farm. We'll do that next week." He nodded. I kissed his white waves of hair. Another precious moment of clarity.

We then went into the family room and sat side by side to watch some TV, as was our habit for the last couple of years. It was *60 Minutes*, and the discussion was on how inaccurate the diagnosis of Alzheimer's had been to that point. In fact, the diagnosis cannot be confirmed until autopsy, post-mortem. The fact was that in over 45 percent of the cases, it was vascular dementia.

Jim repeated, "That's me. It is vascular dementia. I do not want there to be any mention of donations to Alzheimer's society. I don't have it."

Another precious moment of clarity; wow, what gifts. You grasp these moments with such delight. This person you know is there again: the sense of humor, spontaneous smile, and that precious spark of energy that a couple in love share; wow, what a warm glow you feel. That exchange of light, energy, love. Thank you.

Another kiss on that precious forehead. All you can do is try to hear them when they feel no fear and the lucidity comes through. It is truly sweet and heartwarming, but with the invasive process of dementia, it becomes less frequent. It is the same for us all as we near the precipice of the end. It seems as if we "can see clearly now," as the song says.

Listen to their wisdom and have your notebook ready to write down their words. Better still, use your phone to record their last conversations. It will mean so much when you are able to hear them again. We are so fortunate to have such technology now to make this possible.

A moment later, and he was back into a state of distorted reality; once again, you must change your approach. It is such a dance between truth and fiction for them. Who is this person who is around me? Why won't she let me go home? Why can't I just get in the car and drive home? You are my sister. Where is my wife? You are a nice lady, but my wife is not going to like having you in her house. These are part of the questions on the slide to exit from reality.

The next morning, I woke at six o'clock. His hand was so hot in mine. His body was on fire. I felt his chest: burning hot. He wanted to go to the bathroom but could not get up himself. I rolled out of bed and proceeded to take his hands and lead him the twenty steps to the toilet. I wondered about a urinary tract inflection, but there was no odor, no burn. He was too weak to get back, so I practically carried him to the bed across the hall and laid him down. I asked him to stay still, put a cool cloth on him, and grabbed the thermometer. He was 39.9 degrees C already.

We were in trouble.

Tried a few sips of water and more cool cloths. In twenty minutes, it was 40.2.

911 was in order. I called them and kept reassuring him and keeping him oriented to this place.

Within twenty minutes, the ambulance arrived at our farm. Simultaneously, Adena and our grandson arrived; they opened the door to the farmhouse and guided the EMTs upstairs via the narrow, steep steps. I could not leave his side.

I knew these attendants; I had called them many times for other patients. How unreal this time. This time, it was my own husband. No stroke yet, but his temperature regulator was gone; 40.8 and still climbing.

It was now 8 a.m. The ambulance left, and I followed ten minutes later (stopping a moment to put on a dress and lipstick and grab Jim's and my IDs).

For three days, they ran tests and gave him IV meds; unfortunately, they could not give a clear diagnosis. He was resting with medications but still disoriented and sleeping most of the time. We stayed with him continuously, holding vigil.

Finally, after Brenda and I thought he was becoming totally delirious, he woke up and said, "Come here, angel." I moved my chair closer, my face closer to him. He took my face in his hands and said, "You will always be my beautiful angel. I love you forever." His eyes rolled back in his head, the whites were showing, and he never spoke again.

Brenda and I were mesmerized and shocked, simultaneously.

The procedural end then happens. Fixed pupils, no pain response, no Babinski; all signs and symptoms of a cerebral incident. This was the end.

We had often talked of how it would be so humane when our society became enlightened enough to have euthanasia in place so that the exit was less traumatic. I wanted this for him after waiting a few days when we knew scientifically and physiologically that there was no miracle possible.

We had both been raised in the farm environment and respected the fact that this long suffering and painful exit was not civilized, without the tireless advocacy of palliative care professionals who were fighting for the principle of dying with dignity. We treated our animals better than our fellow humans. The legislation was not yet in place, but we could offer progressive pain management; Finally I accepted the inevitability of my spouse's death.

He was moved to the palliative unit, and his likely end of life was projected to be within a few days. I could now be his wife, soon to be widow; others could help me. For seven more days, my darling lay in that bed.

For seven days, we kept vigil. The staff was marvelous. They tended to him, cared for him, turned him, and gave him sedation to help control the involuntary motions of his heaving breaths. Every five seconds, a heave and almost an audible plea of breath, but we could do no more. Was the plea to let him go? Was the plea "I do not want to go"? No food, no fluids, nothing but our love and touch for another seven days was our vigil.

Finally, on Friday afternoon at 4:30, I was standing at the sink in the palliative unit, six floors up; I turned to my right and saw a round globe of light about six inches in diameter enter through the window and come over to me at the sink. It brushed my leg and then slowly moved across the room on an angle, floating over Jim and moving out through the window.

I whispered, "Goodbye, darling."

What a gift; what a sign.

What a message. Our spirit, our soul goes on.

It is released from this physical shell. I prayed and thanked God for this sign.

Death was such a gift after twenty-four hours for eight days: two hundred hours.

The gift of silence came at 4:04 a.m. on May 31.

The gift of death. Rest with peace.

He was home.

The last thing that Jim wanted was to be in a nursing home. He loved to walk the fields of his retirement home, find the calf the cow had hidden in the meter-high hay, and soak up the gentle morning breeze. He would come and bring me out to watch the fireflies when they arrived. We would walk out to the edge of the field and watch them dance amongst the tall grass and the tree branches that whispered a welcome in the night breeze. Then we'd further marvel at the vast magnificence of the millions of stars and God's masterpiece that we are to tend and sustain. How can we ever doubt the presence of a Holy Master in charge?

Jim now had his own wings; like that glowing globe of light, he was free.

See you later in heaven, honey.

13

Share Your Story

SINCE SHARING THIS tale of the orb of light, I have heard it repeated on several deathbed occasions. We must start to tell these stories. We must share them; open the dialogue. There are so many: butterflies that land and stay; cardinals that visit and sing; dimes that are persistently found in the most improbable places; voices that try to reach out; and helium balloons that remain fully inflated for weeks, floating from room to room when company comes to visit, following the death of a grandmother the day after her ninetieth birthday.

But another time, another book. We will share these spirit stories that continue to bring us messages:

1. Fear not; I am with you always.
2. Death is the universal end.
3. Let us dispel the fear; let us talk about it as our final holy journey.

Now we even have options.

14

The Final Gift of Choices

HOW MARVELOUS IT is to be living at this time of our evolution as a species. There are many subtle signs, symptoms, and evidence of our coming evolution. We have long known about racial inequality, greed of food, money, and power. But at present, there is an exaggeration of the frequency of all things. Vibrations are increasing; are we going to respond in time? I believe yes. As a species, our adaptability will be our saving grace, as proven throughout academia, specifically anthropology.

At present, though, many individuals have become silently complacent. They have become cynical and fatigued of debating what is truth; they have isolated themselves off from the mainstream.

Some even isolate themselves in elitist positions, being so mindful that they forget that it takes doing and communicating our optimistic vision or we become an enabler to those who promote fear and seek power through intimidation. The pendulum has swung far in that direction, and it is time that we look beyond the darkness, see past the despair, and think about solutions in the present.

What would we want for ourselves? Remember those words: Love one another as I have loved you.

Do onto others as you would have them do onto you. What would not be fixed?

We have advanced technology; we can communicate worldwide. We can think worldwide. We can solve worldwide. We just must start to do; yes, the first word of the Golden Rule is "Do."

We are evolving. I love this word. It signifies that we are learning our lessons. We are looking at shifting old ways of solving. Take the first four letters and reverse them: love. The collective minds are so powerful when we realize that we are all connected to one another. We have such a responsibility to think in the positive, with visions of a solution. It starts with you.

You are not just eight systems. You are one amazing spirit with eight interconnected systems to keep you operating.

Extrapolate that further.

Imagine how much more information you have gathered into your operating system in the last five years in comparison to an existence three hundred years ago, where you were just trying to stay alive: no phone, no hydro, no cities, no international awareness.

So it is with death of the physical body.

The facts are, when we are born, two cells meet and grow; we live, we start to erode, we die.

What did you do (or what are you going to do) before you leave? Did you add a positive force to our human progress?

Did you see beyond your ego and reach out to add to the one body, our human race?

Did you fulfill the mission that you came here to solve? Did you do something to add to the lives of others? Try writing your own obituary. What do you want it to say? What is your legacy?

While musing over our evolution as a species, I stopped my writing to listen to a full discussion on composting our bodies after death. Yes, I was amazed. It seems we have come full circle. The speaker mentioned that the only country in the world that is still doing this is Tibet. They take their bodies to the forest and compost them amongst the trees, where it becomes fertilizer. It is now available for sale in North America.

Ashes to ashes, dust to dust. We are still finite. We just seem to have a few more options to get there now. Cultures and religions have their own rituals, which I fully respect, but for this discussion, we will examine the options of North America.

The fact is that a ritual of some kind is essential to remediate grief and bereavement. The stages outlined by Kubler-Ross still set the foundation: Denial, Anger, Bargaining, Depression, and Acceptance; this reconciliation or assimilation of the reality that they are gone helps you come to a peaceful place with that fact.

After Jim died, I've had the privilege of leading several grief support groups. These groups have been such an example of the healing power of time and the process of sharing your story over and over to absorb the sensation of loss with every one of your senses. The more often you tell the story to others, the more you can examine your feelings and process them. It is like continuously tilling the soil deeper and deeper, until the joy starts to grow again.

The stories are not all flowers and romance. They are real, and the truths of conflict and the hard work of keeping a relationship going and growing is accepted in the company of others; confidential sharing takes place in what I have labelled our Good Grief Groups (or GGGs).

In this life, we are not promised everything will be perfect. No, that chance ended when Adam and Eve were cast out of the Garden of Eden by disobeying the one command: Do not eat from that Tree of Knowledge.

Ego has always been our downfall.

It continues to be.

When will we get it that we need to get over ourselves?

There is only one unconditional love, and that is who I call God.

I respect that there are many who give that omnipresence many other names, so please insert your own to your comfort. I do adhere to mutual respect. It makes love possible.

Finally, so many have asked the following question: How do you walk into your farmhouse in the dark and deal with there being no one there?

My answer is, "When I walk in, I flick on the light switch and say out loud, 'Hi, God. I'm home.'"

Yes, that is right. I always feel that He is right there with me. I therefore rarely feel alone.

I invite you to do the same.

You do not have to lose your spouse to do this, either.

That is another important thing to remember: We all die alone. I repeat: We all die alone. No one does it for you.

No matter how many are standing around you in your final hour, there is only you doing this at that moment. This is the departure of your spirit from this earthly body. You are moving out and on. In the stories that I have been shown, I have seen it, heard it, and smelled it.

Again, you are returning home, and that is another debate as to what that looks like.

It is your own personal journey to find that out for yourself. You came here with a mission and purpose.

Did you know it? Did you fulfill it?

The gap in the equation is how we die. Our present society does not like to use the words *death* and *dying*. We reframe this inevitable stage with "passed on," or "passed away," and "lost."

What if we could turn death on its ear? What if we looked upon it as a birth gift? It is how we manage it that can ease the missing. We will miss this person's precious energy, their laughter, their physical love, their touch, their sound, their smell, their frequency. But we must continue to address the final moments of their life, rather than ignore them.

Many people on this level of humanity have evolved to a place of knowing that we are spiritual beings on a human journey. It is no longer a requirement that we suffer on our own exit to eternity.

As a Christian, I believe Jesus took responsibility for our stupidity and entreated to His Father, "Forgive them, they know not what they do." He is preparing your landing.

I have heard and seen the spirit being lifted from many bodies; I have sensed a long final sigh. It feels like, "Finally, it is done. My journey is over."

Options for dying are now being addressed in a much more enlightened manner. We have sedatives. We have pain-relieving medications. We have sensible changes in how we manage palliative care. Their mantra is relief of pain and symptoms.

Several states and provinces in North America have the option of medical assistance in dying (MAID). This is another major step in the maturity of our humanity, when we can offer this option to those who face a long journey of intractable pain and inevitable death.

It is not for all because many still hold precious tenets and beliefs based on their personal religion, but at least now, it is an option. The legislation is well thought out and ethical; this choice has been available in Canada since June 2016. But it is your choice.

Since I first sat down to write the outline of the magical steps that allow me to speak so easily of death and dying, much has happened in this area of care. Over ten years ago, I sat in on a seminar in a provincial palliative conference with several lawyers and ethicists, who said they believed it would be almost impossible for euthanasia to happen in our country. Yes, it was happening in Europe and Colorado, but something about the Bill of Rights that would make it next to impossible in Canada.

Well, one of my father's favorite quotes has come true: "There is one thing stronger than the force of a thousand armies, and that is an idea whose time has come."

Yes, the time has come. Medical assistance in death or dying has come to fruition. It is a choice and is being further expanded as people have witnessed the pros and cons and are able to make an informed decision.

It still must be comfortable with your soul. Even if you have all the documentation in place, you can still opt out.

So far, I've been involved in three cases of MAID. I give you the following observations:

1. There are many criteria in place to make assistance in death safe for you.
2. Legally, an assisted death is not considered a suicide (June 2016) in Canada.
3. There are two medical opinions required from independent, nonrelated practitioners that the patient's status is terminal and imminent.

4. The application for a practitioner is fifty-three pages long.
5. The patient must be able to speak the words "that they know that following the injection or medications, they will be dead."
6. In all cases, the emotional relief experienced by the patient allowed them to have a true "face of glory," as they visited with their friends, family, and loved ones.
7. Medication can now be given at a level that alleviates most of the physical pain, so that patients no longer seek refuge under the sheets from pain.
8. The final few days can be spent sharing photo albums, relating fun stories to family, and assisted death goodbyes, not wondering what hour or day the death will happen.
9. Most messages of forgiveness have been resolved.
10. There is time for patients to address their own belief system and possibly teach others.
11. Following the injection of the final sedative, there is a time of peace as their eyes close.
12. After the final injection, the spirit seems to rise; it is as if the body def lates like a balloon and presses against the bed and slides down. You know it is done. It is so quiet and still.
13. Death is the gift. No more pain, no more anguish on exit. All have shared in silence.

All of this can be done in hospice, with meds for pain control, but some cities don't allow terminal MAID. But many know not the hour of exit, so too many times, the option chosen is avoiding the topic.

I further submit the question, what about those who have conditions such as brain death through injury, those with Alzheimer's, to those who suffered a cerebral stroke and lie in bed until an infection ravages their body to death?

Is living helplessly in a fetal position humane? Is that how you want to die? I had the same question fifty years ago with the anencephalic baby.

Is this how you want to let your family witness your death?

I do not know the answers. I just want you to think about it and do something about it.

Finally, the hard question: can we afford this on a human resource basis?

Will we experience a type of pandemic to make us aware of our errors and force us to think of the fragility of life and the inevitability of death?

Is it right? Do we have courage to address the issue? I put these questions out there to think about.

Please think and pray for your God's wisdom and answer.

It is what separates us from robots. We possess a magical spirit of light and energy that can be a beacon of positive powerful change for all humankind.

Sit in peace and tranquility of spirit.

We have tamed the fear of death when we can do this one thing.

Calm the mind to hear your soul speak.

Choose your method: mindfulness, meditation, sleep, hypnotic state, Zen, and prayer.

You choose; they are all there for you.

Imagine on your final moments on this life journey, no fear, that your final thought could be, *Hi, God. I'm home. WOW!*

Wow. Thank you; I am dying. I am coming home. I can rest now; what a gift.

My tombstone already reads "Thanks for the sacred journey of Love and Light."

Keep your wings on.

> "The purpose of life is to live not simply exist. Thus, approach all things with enthusiasm, will, and faith, and the sparkling rivers of life shall surely flow through you."
>
> —Downloaded to my pen at 2 a.m., March 1969,
> Beverly (Bruce) Wilkins, R.N., W.I.P.

ABOUT THE AUTHOR

Beverly Wilkins is a mother, widow, Gamma, friend, grief navigator, palliative nurse, naturopathic doctor, reiki master, minister, author, and a student of the human condition.

Her best description is as a work in progress (WIP). Yes, we are all works in progress, as we try to share one another's losses and loves. Her favorite assignment is to "Love one another as I have loved You."

Imagine how much that would fix in this world. I doubt many of us would assign our only son to die for the rest of us.

Let's relinquish the bondage of fear around dying and instead plan for it with exuberance; make it a celebration that we did not waste our time here on earth so we may rise up in victory to our next birthday celebration with the words "Hi, God. I'm Home. Wow!"

www.ingramcontent.com/pod-product-compliance
Lightning Source LLC
Chambersburg PA
CBHW021451070526
44577CB00002B/356